ALL EYES AND EARS

Rogelio Martinez

BROADWAY PLAY PUBLISHING INC
New York
www.broadwayplaypublishing.com
info@broadwayplaypublishing.com

ALL EYES AND EARS
© Copyright 2010 by Rogelio Martinez

Cover art by Mark Bauhs
First printing: July 2010
I S B N: 978-0-88145-442-0

Book design: Marie Donovan
Typographic controls & page make-up: Adobe InDesign
Typeface: Palatino
Printed and bound in the U S A

ALL EYES AND EARS was commissioned by INTAR
Theater (Eduardo Machado, Artistic Director). The first
performance was on 3 May 2009 with the following
cast and creative contributors:

CARMEN .... Terumi Matthews
EMILIO .... Martin Solá
YOLANDA .... Christina Pumariega
ALVARO .... Liam Torres
STEPAN .... Ed Vassallo
MARIA .... Maria Helan

Director .... Eduardo Machado
Scenic & lighting design .... Maruit Evans
Costume design .... Michael Bevins
Sound design .... Elizabeth Rhodes
Hair & make-up design .... Brenda Bush
Casting .... Billy Hopkins
Press representation .... David Gersten & Associates
Production manager .... Stephanie Madonna
Assistant director .... Meiyin Wang
Production stage manager .... Michael Alifanz
Stage manager .... Hannah Woodward

CHARACTERS & SETTING

CARMEN
EMILIO, *her husband*
YOLANDA, *her daughter, seventeen*
ALVARO
STEPAN, *a Soviet*
MARIA, seventeen

Time: 1961-1962—after the Bay of Pigs and before the Cuban Missile Crisis.

I wish to dedicate the play to Eduardo Machado, teacher and friend.

ACT ONE

Scene One

(*1961*)

(*A book lined living room with three ceiling fans. Downstage is a floor globe. Upstage are three French doors.*)

(*Standing center stage is* CARMEN.)

CARMEN: All right. On three. One. Two. Three.

(*Offstage, from two different locations, we hear toilets being flushed.*)

CARMEN: What happened?

YOLANDA: (*Offstage*) It worked.

CARMEN: How about yours, Emilio? Was there enough pressure?

EMILIO: (*Offstage*) Yes.

CARMEN: Let's try it again.

YOLANDA: (*Offstage*) Oh, come on, Mami!

CARMEN: Oh, come on nada. Ready?

EMILIO: (*Offstage*) La niña is right, Carmen.

CARMEN: What?

EMILIO: (*Offstage*) How long are you going to have us do this?

CARMEN: Just a few more times to make sure—

(YOLANDA, *seventeen, enters. She is dressed like a pionera—red skirt, white shirt, and red kerchief.*)

CARMEN: What are you doing?

YOLANDA: I'm bored.

CARMEN: I want you to go back to where you were.

YOLANDA: You can't make me flush toilets all day long.

CARMEN: Did you hear her, Emilio? She doesn't want to listen to me.

(YOLANDA *plops herself down on a chair.*)

EMILIO: (*Offstage*) Did you say three?

CARMEN: I said she doesn't want to—

(*A toilet is flushed offstage.*)

EMILIO: (*Offstage*) It worked. How about yours, Yoly?

YOLANDA: Perfect.

EMILIO: (*Offstage*) What?

YOLANDA: Perfect!

CARMEN: Now you've gone and confused your father.

YOLANDA: I've been flushing all day. Enough.

CARMEN: (*calling out*) Get in here, Emilio. (*To* YOLANDA) Just because we've moved out of our old home doesn't mean you now get to do what you want.

YOLANDA: We're in the middle of a revolution.

(*A toilet is flushed.*)

CARMEN: Stop with the toilet, Emilio, and get in here.

YOLANDA: My teacher said that the "youth of the revolution are its leaders". Do you know what that means?

CARMEN: Emilio!

YOLANDA: I'm in charge.

(*A toilet is flushed.*)

CARMEN: Emilio! Tell your father to get in here.

YOLANDA: What if I said no?

CARMEN: Emilio!

(EMILIO *enters.*)

CARMEN: She doesn't want to do it anymore.

YOLANDA: I think it's really stupid.

EMILIO: What else do you want, Carmen? We have five toilets and two of them you can flush at the same time. There's nothing else to find out.

CARMEN: You're right. You're right.

EMILIO: I am?

CARMEN: I'm so happy. Come here.

(EMILIO *walks over.*)

CARMEN: You too.

YOLANDA: Do I have to?

CARMEN: Yes.

(YOLANDA *walks over.* CARMEN *hugs them both.*)

CARMEN: This is incredible. They've given us a house. A house with everything and five working toilets. I never thought I'd live in such a house.

(*One ceiling fan comes on.*)

CARMEN: Happiness.

YOLANDA: And my own room—don't forget that.

CARMEN: (*To* EMILIO) And one large bed for us to sleep in.

EMILIO: I was fine where we were.

CARMEN: Ay, Emilio.

YOLANDA: And did you see how many closets—with clothes!

EMILIO: Those are not your clothes.

YOLANDA: They fit me.

EMILIO: They're not yours.

YOLANDA: Mami?

CARMEN: They're not coming back for them.

YOLANDA: They already tried and Fidel went Bang Bang and it was over.

EMILIO: Just wait a few months before you start wearing them.

YOLANDA: For what?

EMILIO: As quickly as they gave us this house they'll take it from us.

YOLANDA: This is the man you married?

CARMEN: This is your father.

YOLANDA: And he was always like this?

EMILIO: Why are you two talking as if I weren't standing here?

YOLANDA: Sometimes it's like you're not.

CARMEN: I wonder what things were said in this room.

YOLANDA: Not much. This was where they read. The reading room. They sat in silence.

(*Silence*)

CARMEN: A room just for reading?

YOLANDA: Someday I'm going to read every one of these books.

EMILIO: Where are you going?

YOLANDA: I want to try my new clothes on.

EMILIO: Can't you wait a few—

YOLANDA: No! (*She exits.*)

EMILIO: (*Calling after her*) Just put them back when you're done.

CARMEN: They're not coming back.

EMILIO: I don't know what I think. I just know this doesn't happen to people like us.

CARMEN: It already did!

EMILIO: Why did they choose you for the job?

CARMEN: Are we going to get into that again?

EMILIO: How can you write reports? You don't even know how to read.

CARMEN: I can read.

EMILIO: You know what I mean. These reports—you need to be a professional reader and writer not just your average reader and writer.

CARMEN: A Revolution has happened. It has made me a professional reader and writer. Understand?

EMILIO: No.

CARMEN: You will.

EMILIO: It just doesn't make sense.

CARMEN: Alvaro says I know more about what's going on in this neighborhood than anyone else.

EMILIO: Fine. But how does that affect national security. It just sounds like they want someone who blabs about their neighbors. They're asking you to be an informant.

CARMEN: How can I be an informant if everyone knows I'm an informant.

EMILIO: What?

CARMEN: Everyone in the neighborhood knows what I do now. They all know who I am. The head of the block committee.

EMILIO: That's what I'm worried about.

CARMEN: You're worried about me getting into trouble.

EMILIO: I'm just worried.

CARMEN: And you were worried the day of the wedding because you didn't think I'd show up.

EMILIO: And you almost didn't.

CARMEN: All right. There you had reason to worry. But now—

EMILIO: You look beautiful.

CARMEN: What?

EMILIO: Against that light just now.

CARMEN: Did you just say—

EMILIO: I did.

CARMEN: You never said things like that in our old home.

EMILIO: It has nothing to do with this house.

CARMEN: Oh, yes it does. In the old house we had two rooms. You couldn't possibly have said that because we had no light. You're going to say more things like that. Emilio!

EMILIO: What?

CARMEN: What were you just thinking about?

EMILIO: Nothing.

CARMEN: I could tell. You left me for a moment.

EMILIO: Ever notice that when you flush the toilet the water goes—

CARMEN: *Ay, Dios mio!*

EMILIO: What am I supposed to be thinking about?
I spent the last half hour flushing a toilet.

CARMEN: Come here!

(CARMEN *grabs* EMILIO *and goes to kiss him.*)

(YOLANDA *enters wearing a beautiful 1950s cocktail dress.*)

YOLANDA: *Oye!*

(CARMEN *and* EMILIO *turn to look at* YOLANDA.)

YOLANDA: I am now a Princess.(*She extends her hand.*)
Come, Papi. Be a gentleman.

(EMILIO *grabs* YOLANDA'*s hand.*)

YOLANDA: *Ay!* Let go.

EMILIO: What do you want?

YOLANDA: Is that how you escort a princess to her seat?
You first lock arms. Gently—barely touching. There.
Now walk me to my seat.

(EMILIO *escorts* YOLANDA *to a seat. She curtsies and he
bows—it's all kind of clumsy.*)

CARMEN: Stand up again.

YOLANDA: A princess is not told what to do.

CARMEN: Stand up!

(YOLANDA *does.*)

CARMEN: Turn around.

EMILIO: What is it?

CARMEN: Come closer.

(YOLANDA *does.*)

CARMEN: I made this dress.

YOLANDA: You did?

CARMEN: It's my stitching.

EMILIO: Are you sure?

CARMEN: My hands are all over this. The ruched pattern was my idea. The old woman wanted it for her niece's confirmation. She needed it done the next day. She'd brought the fabric with her and a picture of Grace Kelly kneeling before the Pope. "Make my niece look like a movie star—only holy."

YOLANDA: It's mine now.

CARMEN: It is yours. I made it. You were always meant to have it.

YOLANDA: That's how this whole thing works. Say something, Papi.

(*Beat*)

CARMEN: She wants you to say something.

(*Beat*)

(*We hear a snippet of* Varadero [Now It's Time For You And Me] *by Carlos Puebla.*)

(*Lights shift. Single light on* CARMEN)

CARMEN: Committee to Defend the Revolution Report. August 15, 1961. For Fidel's birthday celebration we had ninety-eight percent attendance. Felipe Betancourt's wheelchair was still not working and he's waiting for the parts, so I am not including his name in the list below. Also, Margarita Valdez was giving birth so she could not be present, but she did name her son Fidelito. One notable absence was Paco Escambray, but after sending someone to his house it was determined that he had committed suicide earlier that day. I have put him down on the list of excused absences. The remaining five names were unexcused absences.
Rosa Marquez
Toto Hernandez
Tatica Flores
Paco Verde

(*Lights up on* EMILIO)

CARMEN/EMILIO: *Milagros Garcia*

CARMEN: During Fidel's celebration several fireworks failed to go off and Tomas Miguel said that's because they were Russian. It got a good laugh from several people but I wasn't looking in the right direction to know for certain who laughed. I will keep my eye out on people making jokes.

(*Light shift.*)

(*As they do, the record player in the room goes on and plays* Compay Gato *by Los Guaracheros.*)

Scene Two

(*The living room.* EMILIO *looks over the report.*)

EMILIO: This is—this is really...

CARMEN: What?

EMILIO: Well I...

CARMEN: Good?

EMILIO: I didn't say that.

CARMEN: Turn off the music.

EMILIO: How long did it take you to write?

CARMEN: An hour. Not hard when you're telling the truth. (*She turns off the record player.*) You didn't think I could do it.

EMILIO: (*Reading the paper*) Notable absence. Unexcused absences. Long sentences. Very official.

CARMEN: You think so?

EMILIO: You're good. There. I said it. How did you do it?

CARMEN: I just wrote down what I saw.

EMILIO: The language here—these are not your words.

CARMEN: They're Fidel's.

EMILIO: Really?

CARMEN: I looked at some of his speeches. For every word we use he uses five. I just did the same.

EMILIO: You think there'll be trouble?

CARMEN: It seems to have worked just fine for him.

EMILIO: For these people you named—trouble for them.

CARMEN: Ay, Emilio.

EMILIO: Well?

CARMEN: It's just a report. They need to know what's going on.

EMILIO: They want to know. They don't need to know.

(CARMEN *exits*.)

EMILIO: What do you think they're going to do with all these names?

CARMEN: (*Offstage*) File it away somewhere just in case....

EMILIO: In case what?

(CARMEN *returns with a whole bunch of face creams*.)

CARMEN: I saw your friend Flores smoking Lucky Strikes. I purposely left that out.

EMILIO: You can't smoke anymore?

CARMEN: Where's he getting American cigarettes?

EMILIO: His nephew in Miami sends them to him.

CARMEN: And what else is his nephew sending him?

EMILIO: How do I know?

CARMEN: Maybe messages, information.

EMILIO: I don't know. I don't read his letters.

CARMEN: People do.

EMILIO: Who? (*Silence*) Who reads his letters?

CARMEN: I'm not going to say anything because he's your friend, but I think you need to tell him to stop doing that. (*She's putting on face cream.*)

EMILIO: What's on your face?

CARMEN: There are all these creams in the bathroom—must have been left behind. They all belong to an Elizabeth Arden—maybe a family friend. Do you know her?

(EMILIO *shakes his head no.*)

CARMEN: I thought you would—someone you had maybe met one night.

EMILIO: You know the people I know.

CARMEN: I want to be sure. That's why I asked you.

EMILIO: You look awful.

CARMEN: That's how it works. Look awful at night so that you can look beautiful in the morning.

EMILIO: I want you beautiful at night.

CARMEN: It's not a perfect system.

EMILIO: It used to be.

CARMEN: What?

EMILIO: You wouldn't look awful at night.

CARMEN: Are you ready? (*She starts to turn off the lights to the room.*)

EMILIO: You're going to bed looking like that?

CARMEN: You don't do anything in bed. You close your eyes, so what does it matter how I look.

EMILIO: Do you feel strange?

CARMEN: Why?

EMILIO: I stayed at a hotel once and I couldn't sleep thinking about all the people that had slept on that one bed before me.

CARMEN: When were you in a hotel?

EMILIO: For my grandfather's funeral in Matanzas.

CARMEN: You could afford a hotel?

EMILIO: You're asking me a lot of questions.

CARMEN: All right. Come to bed. You have to drive the bus tomorrow.

EMILIO: I haven't slept in two weeks. When you fall asleep I just get up and walk around. I walk around and eventually I fall asleep in a chair in the servant's kitchen.

CARMEN: Why?

EMILIO: I want to get rid of that bed.

CARMEN: And where are we going to get another one?

EMILIO: I don't know.

CARMEN: You want to move somewhere else?

EMILIO: I didn't say that.

CARMEN: Maybe if you...if we...

(CARMEN *tries coming on to* EMILIO. *It's awkward. He tries. Then...*)

EMILIO: Maybe.

CARMEN: Maybe tonight?

EMILIO: Not tonight.

CARMEN: I don't know what you want. (*She exits.*)

EMILIO: I'm going to sit outside for a while—wait for the train to pass.

(EMILIO *goes to exit through the French doors. Suddenly all the lights come back on and so does the record player. He rushes back and turns off the record player.*)

(*Lights shift.*)

Scene Three

(*A light on* YOLANDA. *She is dressed in another gorgeous cocktail dress. She reads a letter that she has obviously read several times.*)

YOLANDA: Dearest Comrade Yolandita. I worry day and night about you. After C I A attack on your country I was worried I never hear from you again. But your people are brave and can fight any challenge. Even when your own people become traitors and attack, you fight challenge. When I read in school history of Bolsheviks I think of your people. How you have fought the evil American empire and succeeded. Today I joined a group of students and we went to harvest wheat. The experience was fulfilling and it allowed me to understand physics better.

(*Suddenly* YOLANDA *sees* EMILIO *standing there.*)

YOLANDA: How long have you been standing there?

EMILIO: Who wrote that?

YOLANDA: A friend.

EMILIO: What friend?

YOLANDA: In school they asked us to write to someone like ourselves in the Soviet Union.

EMILIO: And he wrote back?

YOLANDA: Yes. It's part of the friendship we've made.

(*A picture falls from the envelope.*)

EMILIO: What is that?

YOLANDA: Nothing.

EMILIO: Let me see.

YOLANDA: It's a picture. *Nada mas.*

EMILIO: A picture is part of the friendship.

YOLANDA: It's a very close friendship.

EMILIO: What's he doing in it?

YOLANDA: He's plowing snow.

EMILIO: There's so much of it.

YOLANDA: Yes. He loves the fact that it never stops. It gives him something to do always. Don't you see how happy he is?

EMILIO: He's not smiling.

YOLANDA: *Que?*

EMILIO: He's grinding his teeth. I think he's very cold.

YOLANDA: In Russia they smile differently. That's how my teacher explained it.

EMILIO: That's because they've forgotten how to smile.

YOLANDA: He's not cold. Look at the hat. He promised to send me one. Everyone in the military gets a Ushanka hat so that the body stays warm when confronting the cold front of capitalism. He says we too will feel a cold front soon.

EMILIO: (*Handing her back the picture*) You should be in bed.

YOLANDA: I'm not tired. I'm going to read. (*She picks up a book from the shelf.*)

EMILIO: You shouldn't touch their stuff.

YOLANDA: Here's a pretty book. I'll read this one. *A Social History of the Luddites.* (*She puts it back.*)

Not this one.

(YOLANDA *puts it back but not in the same place.* EMILIO *fixes it.*)

EMILIO: That's not yours.

YOLANDA: It is mine. Everything here is mine. (*She takes the book and puts it back incorrectly.*)

EMILIO: I found pictures of her—the girl who lived here. A whole album of pictures from when she was little.... I found a picture of her wearing that same dress. I want you to wear something that's yours.

YOLANDA: Here's a good one. *Gulliver's Travels.*

EMILIO: Do you ever hear things?

YOLANDA: What do you mean?

EMILIO: In the house?

YOLANDA: Like what?

EMILIO: Not sure.

YOLANDA: You think the people who owned this place are going to come back?

EMILIO: No but— ...well not sure.

(YOLANDA *takes off her shoe.*)

EMILIO: What are you doing?

(YOLANDA *smacks her shoe down on the table.*)

YOLANDA: (*In her best Russian accent*) "Whether you like it or not, history is on our side. We will bury you!"

EMILIO: Are you out of your mind?

(YOLANDA *smacks her shoe down once again.*)

EMILIO: You're going to break that.

YOLANDA: I am practicing my Russian accent. It's for the school play. This year I have volunteered to play Khrushchev. How do I sound? I am going to wear two big pillows under my suit. "Whether you like it or not, history is on our side. We will bury you!" Well?

EMILIO: You sound just like him.

YOLANDA: You know just what to say.

(CARMEN *enters.*)

CARMEN: What's going on?

YOLANDA: Doesn't anybody sleep in this house?

CARMEN: Not with you banging on things.

YOLANDA: I was showing Papi my very best Khruschev. You want to see?

(CARMEN *hesitates.*)

YOLANDA: "Whether you like it or not, history is on our side. We will bury you!"

(*Several books tip over—not necessarily the ones closest to where she slams down.*)

YOLANDA: What do you think?

(CARMEN *is stunned for a moment.* EMILIO *elbows her.*)

EMILIO: Just like Khruschev.

CARMEN: Yeah. Just like him. (*She hugs her parents— Khruschev style.*)

Come on. Come on. Off to bed.

YOLANDA: Good night. (*She exits.*)

EMILIO: She gets letters from a Russian boy.

CARMEN: I know.

EMILIO: You do?

CARMEN: I have Militina intercept them at the post office. Harmless letters. Mostly he talks about how wonderful life is in Moscow. (*She looks out the window.*)

EMILIO: Our daughter is the one you should really keep an eye on.

CARMEN: What's she going to do?

EMILIO: She's confused about what revolution means. (*Beat*) Are you listening to me?

CARMEN: Her and the rest of us, Emilio. Everyone is a little confused right now and so what. Every day we are better off than the last. That's all that matters. (*Beat*) Come back to bed with me.

EMILIO: You know how you can feel your own heartbeat when you lie down. When I'm lying down in that bed I feel someone else's heartbeat on top of mine.

CARMEN: No you don't.

EMILIO: Yes I do. Someone's in that bed with me.

CARMEN: I'm in that bed with you.

EMILIO: Someone else.

CARMEN: No one else should be in that bed with you.

EMILIO: We've taken someone's house and they're not happy, Carmen. A ghost.

CARMEN: Do you understand that to be a ghost you first have to be dead? The people who lived here are not dead, they're in Hialeah.

EMILIO: Maybe they're coming back.

CARMEN: Nobody who's left for Hialeah is allowed to come back.

EMILIO: Sometimes I have nightmares that I'm lying in bed and their whole family is standing in front of me at the foot of the bed. I open my eyes in my dream and they ask me what I'm doing.

CARMEN: And next time that happens you tell them to go away, that you're sleeping.

EMILIO: I try to say something to them but they have a lawyer with them.

CARMEN: The family from Hialeah has a lawyer with them?

EMILIO: Yeah.

CARMEN: You're having nightmares involving lawyers?

EMILIO: *Uno solo.* He speaks for the entire family. He tells me this is not my bed and that I need...he uses a very specific word.

CARMEN: What is it?

EMILIO: I don't know. It's a word only a lawyer understands and because I can't afford a lawyer I'm left speechless.

CARMEN: And then what happens?

EMILIO: Then I wake up.

CARMEN: You need to start dreaming with the right kind of lawyers.

EMILIO: What kind are those?

CARMEN: The ones that give you things and not take things from you. People forget that Fidel is a lawyer. And he told us this house belongs to us.

EMILIO: That's just it. For us to have something, someone else had to lose it.

CARMEN: For us to have had nothing—which is what we had—someone else had to have had a hell of a lot.

EMILIO: I don't understand.

CARMEN: They had five toilets, Emilio. Do you think that's right?

EMILIO: But now we have—

CARMEN: Marxist economics don't always make sense at two in the morning. *Vamos.*

EMILIO: You're not a Marxist.

CARMEN: Yes I am.

ACT ONE 19

EMILIO: You didn't know what a Marxist was until last year.

CARMEN: It means all good things for us.(*She takes his hand.*)

(*A train is heard offstage.*)

EMILIO: Like clockwork.

(*Train is heard louder now.*)

(*Lights shift.*)

Scene Four

(*The sounds of an assembly*)

(ALVARO *and* STEPAN *walk on stage.* STEPAN *stands to the side.*)

ALVARO: *Compañeros. Compañeros.* There are some seats over there. Over on the left. Good. Good. Today, December 18th 1961, marks a turning point in the history of the Revolution. I have very exciting news to share with you. I've heard your suggestions and spoken to District Leader Manolo Perez who has passed on the information to Comandante Mateo Sanchez in La Habana and today we take the first step toward a new society. A new society where women move from the home to the workforce. Where the woman stands next to the man. I want to share a few sketches I was able to do in my office. (*He pulls down a poster.*)
   This is a sketch of the 1957 Housewife. As you can see her hair is put up with toilet paper rolls in the fashion of the time. This is a sketch of what the 1966 Housewife will look like. (*He pulls down a second sketch. It's a blank piece of paper.*) *Compañeros*, the idea of the housewife will not exist in 1966. In her place there will be... (*He pulls down another sketch. On it a woman is*

dressed in military green and looking quite intimidating.)

The revolutionary woman. With her fatigues and black boots, if there's one word that describes her, strong, empowered, in control, dominant, with discipline, focus, dangerous, alert...that may be more than one word.

Compañeros, we now have a five year plan to get from this to that. So how do we do it? Through a variety of studies that we've conducted over the past six months we've come to understand one basic problem. On stage with me is Comrade Stepan Bakunin. He has brought with him The Petronov Industrial Washer/Dryer set from Moscow. (*He pulls down a picture of a washer/dryer.*)

The Soviet Union has given us this great gift to help us begin to take the leap forward. Comrade Bakunin will spend the next few weeks visiting you, living with you, observing you, teaching you how to work this very important washer/dryer gift.

We understand from our studies that the one thing above all others that keeps women at home are household chores. These machines will be a step in eliminating the time it takes to do the wash. In the new Patrice Lumumba Center.(*He pulls down a picture of a new building, but this last pull causes it to fall.*) *Coño.*

(CARMEN *gets up to help. As she walks across the stage, we hear general whistling and noise.*)

ALVARO: Thank you, *compañera.*

CARMEN: You're welcome, *compañero.*

ALVARO: Here. In this building we're setting up not only a daycare but we will make these good machines available so that women can come, wash their clothes, and quickly return to the workplace. (*He pulls down a final image. It is of the 1957 housewife next to the 1966 revolutionary woman standing in front of the Patrice Lumumba Center and next to them the washer/dryer.*)

Soon we will officially take charge of eight of these new machines in a ceremony to be conducted in Serafin Sanchez Park. We must prepare for the transformation that will begin to happen shortly after. It is your job as representatives of the Committee to Defend the Revolution to go to your individual neighborhoods and explain to your neighbors what this means and the change that is coming for both women and men. If you have any questions? Good. *Patria o Muerte.*

AUDIENCE: *Venceremos!*

(*Blackout*)

Scene Five

(*The living room.* CARMEN *is there looking at a piece of paper. Standing over her is* STEPAN. ALVARO *stands to one side.*)

(*Beat*)

CARMEN: What am I looking at?

STEPAN: You're looking at the numbers.

CARMEN: These are the numbers?

STEPAN: Those are the numbers. Look at the next page.

CARMEN: More numbers.

ALVARO: The 1957 numbers.

CARMEN: What am I looking at now?

STEPAN: More numbers.

CARMEN: But what do they mean?

STEPAN: What do you mean what do they mean?

ALVARO: She wants to know what the numbers mean.

(STEPAN *looks around, suspiciously.*)

STEPAN: There's growth. In 1957 look at numbers then and now. Now explosion.

CARMEN: And that's good right?

ALVARO: The birth rate has tripled in this province alone.

CARMEN: It's very good?

STEPAN: It is a very bad thing. Russian woman is working woman. And working woman must decide for herself the number of babies she can, how do I say, make most of. Cuban is now Russian and Russian is now Cuban. And Cuban woman must now decide when to have baby and when to not. This country has been too much under other influences. In order to build communism we give you washing machines but we also tell you that your future is not at home but at work. At work with other people building revolutionary machine. We make it possible.

CARMEN: I don't know what you want.

ALVARO: La Habana is looking carefully at provinces where the birth rate continues to go up. We want to reach out to women...to let them know there are other options beyond the family. That now you have a bigger family.

STEPAN: The family of man.

ALVARO: Correct.

STEPAN: We beat Americans to space but they were smart and went directly to bedroom.

(YOLANDA *enters with a tray and three cups of café.*)

(STEPAN *walks up to* YOLANDA. *Immediately,* CARMEN *rises and takes the tray with the café.* YOLANDA *exits.*)

STEPAN: In 1948 United States found out what was happening with their citizens in bedroom in Kinsey

Report. This is copy of Kinsey Report—all essential facts have been underlined.

ALVARO: I've spent many restless nights reading that terrible book—there's so much I now know about the immoral American mind. It is filthy.

STEPAN: Filthy.

(CARMEN *reaches for it. He stops her.*)

ALVARO: This thing has the power to corrupt you. Careful with it.

(CARMEN *smiles at* ALVARO.)

(*Beat*)

(CARMEN takes the book and leafs through it.)

STEPAN: We want to know more about what happens in bedroom. We want for you to tell us.

ALVARO: Your position in town as a member of the block committee carries great influence. Keep that in mind. Use that influence in the bedroom.

STEPAN: We want to help woman so she can make correct choice. A child is not only choice when building Revolution.

ALVARO: Let's see if we can start to bring these numbers down. Make the woman understand that her place is in the workforce and not home taking care of children. You must help us do that.

STEPAN: We're helping you build society that you can afford. Too many babies becomes too much money. Moscow does not believe these numbers are affordable long term.

ALVARO: Understand what he's saying? Good.

(CARMEN *continues to leaf through the report.*)

ALVARO: Are you all right, *compañera*?

CARMEN: Are these numbers right?

STEPAN: In my limited dealings with Americans I can testify to all numbers in the Kinsey report being completely correct.

CARMEN: Forty percent of men like sex with the lights on?

STEPAN: Complete waste of electric power.

CARMEN: Thirty percent of men have...

ALVARO: What is it?

CARMEN: Oh.

STEPAN: Filthy men.

(CARMEN *closes it.*)

CARMEN: How is this report supposed to help me?

ALVARO: The report is to encourage you to walk through the bedroom door—to understand that things are said in the bedroom, done in the bedroom that we may need to know about.

STEPAN: Your enemy may lie next to you and only in that moment of passion does he reveal himself fully.

ALVARO: Do you know who Alain Delon is?

CARMEN: The enemy?

ALVARO: What are you doing tonight?

CARMEN: My husband will be home—

ALVARO: Don't say another word. You're in for a wonderful surprise.

STEPAN: I want you to spend the night with us.

CARMEN: What?

ALVARO: Tonight we're watching a French movie. I don't want to say too much. There's a dinner

beforehand in honor of Stepan. I want you to join us as
our guest.

STEPAN: American mind is easily corruptible.

(*Blackout*)

Scene Six

(YOLANDA *lies on the sofa. She is breathlessly reading a
letter. Quietly, the record player plays a bolero.*)

YOLANDA: (*Reading*)

"Dearest Comrade Yolandita, I received your letter
with record. I listen to song number nine. It is driving
crazy. Why is so small a country driving me into
lunatic place. How is my Spanish? Do I write better.
I am hot for you. Those are only words I now need to
learn. I don't make sense. I plow a lot of snow. Then I
come back in and I listen to record and think of you.
I walk out and there's new snow and I plow again.
Then I walk back in and listen to record and think of
you. That is what my life has become. I do it five times
a day. Send me more records, more letters. I will take
your letters, look for your scent, I will find you in
letters, I will—"

EMILIO: (*Offstage*) I won! Yolandita! Yolanda? Hey.
I have good news!

(YOLANDA *quickly puts the letter away and rushes to turn
off the music but* EMILIO *is there. He has his beat up lunch
box and pool cue.*)

EMILIO: That was your mother's favorite bolero.

YOLANDA: What happened?

EMILIO: She stopped playing it.

YOLANDA: No. You said you had good news.

EMILIO: I'm going to tell you.

YOLANDA: What is it?

EMILIO: Here comes my favorite part.

(YOLANDA *stops the record.*)

EMILIO: Your mother was beautiful when I met her.

YOLANDA: She still is. Now what happened?

EMILIO: I won. This guy I never saw before was there. We were shooting pool. Had the eight ball right across—except the five ball was in the way. Boom. Jumped the five. Eight ball corner pocket. Smooth. Yolandita, I won.

YOLANDA: That's exciting. What did you win?

EMILIO: I just won.

YOLANDA: But what was the prize.

EMILIO: There wasn't any. I won.

YOLANDA: You didn't win anything?

EMILIO: I won the game.

YOLANDA: But if you'd lost you'd still be the same.

EMILIO: I would have lost.

YOLANDA: What would you have lost? (*Pause*) Nothing. What did you win?

EMILIO: Nothing.

YOLANDA: I'm going to bed.

EMILIO: I don't like to feel like a loser.

YOLANDA: You're not. You won. (*She starts to go.*)

EMILIO: What's happened to you?

YOLANDA: What do you mean?

EMILIO: I don't know. I think you're acting differently.

YOLANDA: I feel different.

EMILIO: How?

YOLANDA: Just. Different. (*Beat*) Sit down.

EMILIO: You want me to sit down?

YOLANDA: You want to talk?

EMILIO: About what?

YOLANDA: You asked me how I felt.

EMILIO: Are you sure you don't want to wait for your mother?

YOLANDA: (*Frustrated*) Good night.

EMILIO: Wait.

YOLANDA: What?

(*Pause*)

EMILIO: Let's talk about it. Soon.

(YOLANDA *exits.*)

(EMILIO *takes his cue and lines up the cue ball in his mind. He strikes the imaginary ball. At that same moment, a tiny little frame falls over and a sound is heard. He is surprised by this. He walks up to the frame. Just then* CARMEN *enters.*)

CARMEN: What are you doing?

EMILIO: Where were you?

CARMEN: At a meeting.

EMILIO: The whole night?

CARMEN: I went to the movies afterwards.

EMILIO: What's playing?

CARMEN: I don't remember what it was called.

EMILIO: You just finished watching it.

CARMEN: It was Alain Delon, a group of women, and a really big swimming pool. It was in French and there were no subtitles.

EMILIO: What's that word you said first?

CARMEN: Alain Delon?

EMILIO: Yes.

CARMEN: French movie star. He smokes cigarettes and wears sweaters. I love sweaters.

EMILIO: Why did you go to the movies alone?

CARMEN: I wasn't alone.

EMILIO: Yolandita was here tonight.

CARMEN: I have friends.

(*Beat*)

EMILIO: Who was there?

CARMEN: Alvaro and Stepan, a Soviet diplomat. They both wanted to show me the dangers of excess when you live in a world where all you care about is yourself.

EMILIO: So they took you to see a movie?

CARMEN: Stepan whispered in my ear quotes from Lenin all during the movie. "Crime is a product of social excess." In one scene, Alain Delon takes off his sweater and Stepan whispered, "The best way to destroy the capitalist system is to debauch the currency." I learned so much today.

EMILIO: All you really remember is one French actor?

CARMEN: I'm going to have to go back and see it again. There's a lot to learn from French cinema.

EMILIO: I thought you'd be home when I got home.

CARMEN: Why?

EMILIO: You usually are.

CARMEN: I have responsibilities.

EMILIO: Going to the movies?

CARMEN: You have no idea what's happening in the world.

EMILIO: It's a movie.

CARMEN: The Soviet man said that movies are a mirror to the way a society wants to be looked at. He wants to take me to the movies again on Thursday. A private screening. They are showing a print of the American film *Gidget*. It is about summer and surfing. With these two movies I can begin to understand the mind of the enemy.

EMILIO: Those two movies have nothing to do with our world.

CARMEN: But they are true and honest about their world.

EMILIO: Fine. I'm just saying—

CARMEN: We each have lives now. I'm not going to be here all the time. And starting in 1966 I will be here even less.

EMILIO: 1966?

CARMEN: Yes.

EMILIO: That's five years from now.

CARMEN: Yes it is. So start planning.

EMILIO: What's going to happen in 1966?

CARMEN: Women will become full time members of the workforce.

EMILIO: In 1966?

CARMEN: Yes. It's part of a five year plan. So now exploit me while you still have the chance—what do you want to eat?

EMILIO: Exploit you? I don't exploit you.

CARMEN: Well...

EMILIO: What?(*Beat*) This Soviet guy told you I exploit you?

CARMEN: You exploit everybody.

EMILIO: Me?

CARMEN: Men. But it's changing. What if I make you an omelet?

EMILIO: And how about the other guy.

CARMEN: Alvaro.

EMILIO: How does Alvaro exploit you?

CARMEN: He doesn't. He's head of the transition committee—he's responsible for the leap.

EMILIO: What leap?

CARMEN: From the home to the workplace.

EMILIO: He's in charge of it?

CARMEN: Don't be so jealous of a man who is so free from the traps laid out by the previous society.

EMILIO: I don't even know what you're saying.

CARMEN: You want to know what I'm saying? Are you sure? According to these numbers we are not normal.

EMILIO: What is that?

CARMEN: More people have sex now than in 1958. It's the other way around for us.

EMILIO: What?

CARMEN: Remember what a great year 1958 was for us. Sex everywhere. We couldn't take our hands off each other. There's an American report—two point six times a week average. Now we're not even average, Emilio.

EMILIO: Two point six what?

CARMEN: Sex.

EMILIO: You're not making any sense.

CARMEN: In America that's average. I want to be average.

EMILIO: We're not in America.

CARMEN: I want at least two point two. I've looked through this report. I now know how the rest of the world lives.

EMILIO: The only thing your job does is give you permission to look into other people's business.

CARMEN: For ideological reasons.

EMILIO: There's no arguing with you.

CARMEN: Our marriage is in trouble.

EMILIO: Says who?

CARMEN: This man Kinsey. And Alvaro. And the Soviet guy.

EMILIO: You spoke to three different people about our marriage?

CARMEN: In a way.

EMILIO: They all told you the same thing?

CARMEN: I'm not even sure you still love me. And before I couldn't really see that but now that I'm looking at what average is...now I know that there's something wrong with us. There's another woman.

EMILIO: No.

CARMEN: Who is it?

EMILIO: It'd be your job to find out, wouldn't it?

CARMEN: Yes it would.

EMILIO: Then find out. Write it up and file it away. I'm going to bed. (*He starts to go.*)

CARMEN: I will find out!

EMILIO: Fine!

CARMEN: Wait!

EMILIO: What?

CARMEN: Do you want food or not?

EMILIO: I bought a sandwich at work.

CARMEN: Oh.

EMILIO: You forgot to put my lunch in the lunchbox. I went to eat and there was nothing there. All the men around me, their wives still care.

CARMEN: I still care.

EMILIO: Do you?

CARMEN: I'm sorry that I have more things to do than most people.

EMILIO: My friend Flores...they came for him a few days ago. To ask him questions. To ask him about his nephew. They asked him about his cigarettes. Afterwards they took all his cigarettes.

CARMEN: And?

EMILIO: I kept hoping he would come talk to me afterwards. Everyone avoids me now because they're too afraid of being themselves. I'm alone. (*Beat*) You have no idea where this will end.

CARMEN: I understand where we're headed. 1966 is just around the corner. You blink you'll miss all the changes.

EMILIO: What changes? The other day at work we got a box from Leningrad—had chains in it. It took us a whole day to figure out the chains were snow tire chains. Snow, Carmen? When was the last time it snowed here?! That's what life is like now. We are in business with a country whose culture, whose language we will never understand. They will never understand us. I might as well have used to chains to tie myself up permanently.

CARMEN: You're not looking at the good things. Look at the neighborhood we live in—this house. We were never even allowed to look at it much less walk through its doors.

EMILIO: I'm getting tired of this house. I have to walk half a mile to go from our room to the toilet down the hall. I can't get used to things being so big.

CARMEN: You're a little upset but that's because you haven't eaten anything.

EMILIO: The people who lived in this house had no idea where it would end. They were as much in the dark as you are now.

CARMEN: We're going to start talking about those people again?

EMILIO: I try to forget and then there they are.

(YOLANDA *enters wearing a different cocktail dress.*)

YOLANDA: I wanted to show you this one. It was bought in El Encanto. The family went one week to La Habana not on vacation but simply to go shopping. Can you imagine? Just to go shopping. I found her diary and she talks about this dress. She says this is the dress she'll wear when she hosts her first party in her own home. Well?

CARMEN: It's a very nice dress.

YOLANDA: No. You're not hearing me. I want to have a party.

CARMEN: What kind of party?

YOLANDA: A party to take possession of this house once and for all.

EMILIO: What?

YOLANDA: If there's anything here that shouldn't be here it'll go away on its own once we have the party.

EMILIO: What makes you think that?

CARMEN: She's right. We've been living as guests in our own home. This is ours. It needs to start feeling like it.

YOLANDA: I'm going to go pick out the perfect necklace. (*She goes.*)

CARMEN: What are you afraid of?

EMILIO: What makes you think I'm afraid of something.

CARMEN: I see the way you walk around this place.

(*Beat*)

EMILIO: Have you noticed this before?

CARMEN: What is it?

EMILIO: It's a picture of a young girl.

CARMEN: I hadn't noticed it before. I'll put it away with the others.

(CARMEN *goes to grab the picture but* EMILIO *keeps it.*)

EMILIO: Yesterday when I left I forgot my wallet— halfway down the block I turned around. I thought I saw someone walking around the house.

CARMEN: Did you?

EMILIO: The family that lived here—it was a big family. But I think I saw a girl Yolanda's age walking around the outside of the house...trying the door. Not getting in.

CARMEN: Did you say anything?

EMILIO: I stopped right where I was and just watched. She eventually walked around the back and I didn't see her return. Did you see anything today?

CARMEN: It could have been anyone.

EMILIO: Yes, yes. It could have been anyone.

CARMEN: But you don't believe that.

EMILIO: I think it's the girl who lived here. I think she came back.

CARMEN: Just forget people ever lived here.

EMILIO: Then tell Yolanda to stop wearing her dresses.

CARMEN: But—

EMILIO: If you want her to leave—

CARMEN: You really think she's here?

EMILIO: Just get her to stop wearing the dresses. (*He exits holding on to the picture.*)

(*Lights shift.*)

(*Music:* La Guarapachanga *is heard loud.*)

Scene Seven

(*The song is now heard coming from another room along with the sounds of a party.*)

(STEPAN *is alone on stage. After a moment,* YOLANDA *enters in a gorgeous dress. She is holding a large spoon.*)

STEPAN: Ah, there before me a Romanov!

YOLANDA: What is a Romanov?

STEPAN: A very special person.

YOLANDA: This is for you.

STEPAN: What is it?

YOLANDA: Mami made borscht. Try it.

(STEPAN *does.*)

STEPAN: Very good. In basement of Kremlin there
is special cafeteria. There is one cafeteria for the
employees of the Kremlin but there's one second
cafeteria for the people who are there but are not
supposed to be there.

YOLANDA: I don't understand.

(*Offstage we no longer hear the music but there are still the
faint sounds of a party.*)

STEPAN: I work for Kremlin but it is not always right
for everyone to know so this special cafeteria has
special entrance and it serves special food. The woman
who runs cafeteria was cook to Imperial family. She is
very old now but she still works for the Soviet people
trying to make up for twenty years of service to the
Czar. She makes delicious borscht. Every time I eat
there I understand I am now connected to royal family.
I am now special. I am now Romanov.

YOLANDA: May I have the spoon back?

STEPAN: What?

YOLANDA: The spoon.

STEPAN: Oh.

YOLANDA: Do I tell her you liked it?

STEPAN: Yes.

YOLANDA: I will tell her it's approved by one who has
been to special cafeteria in Kremlin.

STEPAN: Good.

(YOLANDA *turns to go.*)

STEPAN: I have had so much of borscht my whole life
that sometimes I feel my skin turning red—even when
I'm not looking at beautiful woman. (*He touches her
hand for a moment.*)

(CARMEN *enters.*)

CARMEN: Another half hour and the *lechon* will be ready.

(CARMEN *exits pushing* YOLANDA *out with her. For a moment* STEPAN *is left alone on stage. Then* YOLANDA *returns.*)

(*Beat*)

STEPAN: Will you dance with me?

YOLANDA: There's no music.

STEPAN: Then we choose song and let it play in our head. I will whisper how song goes now and we dance. Understand?

(STEPAN *goes to whisper but kisses* YOLANDA *instead. Immediately, she kisses him back. Then he leads her in a waltz.*)

(YOLANDA *stops.*)

YOLANDA: I must tell you right now that my heart belongs to a Soviet boy who has been writing me letters.

STEPAN: Tell me his name and I will have him sent to gulag at sunrise.

YOLANDA: His name is Nicholas Petrovich and he lives in Promyshlennyi.

STEPAN: (*Correcting her pronunciation*) Promyshlennyi, Vorkuta Province. Done.

YOLANDA: Will he be getting a promotion of some kind?

STEPAN: Oh yes. Of some kind. Now allow me the dance.

(STEPAN *and* YOLANDA *continue to dance.*)

(ALVARO *and* EMILIO *enter. They're drinking.* EMILIO *is drunk. The men are laughing.*)

(ALVARO *and* EMILIO *watch* STEPAN *and* YOLANDA
dance.)

(*Suddenly,* YOLANDA *becomes aware of everyone watching.
She stops, embarrassed. They all clap.*)

ALVARO: I had no idea you would be able to dance so
well.

STEPAN: I was ballet dancer when only five. Broke my
two legs—different times. Lost all strength. Now I
use my strengths to fight American imperialism but
sometimes I dance.

ALVARO: I was complimenting the young woman.

STEPAN: Ah.

(YOLANDA *curtsies.*)

STEPAN: I want you now to dance different dance. With
this dance I remember youth. Everyone. Clap.

(*They start to clap hesitantly.*)

STEPAN: No. Like this.

(STEPAN *claps vigorously and the others follow.*)

(CARMEN *enters.*)

CARMEN: What's everyone doing in here? The rest of
the guests are going to be arriving soon.

STEPAN: Come Carmen. Dance with me.

CARMEN: I have to get ready for—

STEPAN: Dance.

CARMEN: I don't know how.

STEPAN: It's easy. Just surrender to the fact that you
will probably make a fool of yourself but you and the
people you are with will be having so good of a time
doing it doesn't matter.

(STEPAN *takes* CARMEN *and grabs onto one of her hands. They dance a wild Russian dance. Eventually she steps to the side and he takes over.*)

(STEPAN *finishes exhausted but exhilarated.*)

(EMILIO *refills his glass.*)

EMILIO: That's the last of the rum. I trust that the State will have more for me soon.

(ALVARO *and* STEPAN *each reach inside their coat pocket and take out smaller bottles of rum and vodka respectively.*)

ALVARO: Is that soon enough?

*(*EMILIO *takes a shot back and reaches out for more.)*

CARMEN: Slow down.

EMILIO: Why? There always seems to be more than enough.

CARMEN: You still should—

EMILIO: "From each according to his ability, to each according to his need." My daughter taught me that. Is that a fair statement to make? "From each according to his ability, to each according to his need."

STEPAN: It is what we all believe.

EMILIO: I am a very needy man. (*He drinks more.*)

STEPAN: Maybe your daughter has not taught you the full extent of what Marx had to say about that.

EMILIO: You mean Marx had more to say?

STEPAN: Yes.

EMILIO: I thought Marx was a man of few words and one idea.

STEPAN: Marx says, "In a higher phase of communist society," then he explains what that is and he concludes, `after productive forces have also increased with all-around development of the individual, and all the springs of co-operative wealth flow more abundantly—only then can the narrow horizon of bourgeois right be crossed in its entirety and society inscribe on its banners: *(In Russian then repeated in English)* "From each according to his ability, to each according to his needs!'" You're not yet at a higher phase of communist society. You're only at the beginning. You have a strong ally and someone who is paving the way for you but do not assume that it will be easy.

EMILIO: You had to go and say all that to ask me to slow down my drinking.

(Pause. No one knows quite what to do or say next.)

STEPAN: It seems Marx has momentarily taken the air out of the room. I apologize. Ah, before I forget.

CARMEN: Hold that thought. I have to go lower the heat.*(She exits quickly.)*

(STEPAN spots the floor globe.)

STEPAN: Ah, this is very nice. *(He spins the globe, violently.)* This is speed we're all moving at. Maybe you suffer from a little motion sickness. Is that the problem? *(He continues to spin the globe, fast.)* Maybe you need some time away. Time for you to make sense of everything again. *(He stops the globe from spinning.)* This globe is not up to date.

YOLANDA: What's wrong with it?

STEPAN: There's no Soviet Union. I do not exist.

YOLANDA: Really?

STEPAN: Come look. Latvia is its own country.

ALVARO: This issue must be resolved immediately. People are going to be coming to this party, wandering around. No member of the C D R can have something like this in their house. (*He removes the globe from the stand and exits with it.*)

YOLANDA: Are you all right?

EMILIO: Yeah.

YOLANDA: What's wrong?

(ALVARO *enters.*)

ALVARO: Problem solved. I hid it in a closet.

EMILIO: Once again you have taught us something valuable.

STEPAN: And what is that?

EMILIO: Now none of us exist.

(CARMEN *reenters.*)

CARMEN: Almost ready and no one's here. What was the surprise?

(STEPAN *takes out a nesting doll.*)

STEPAN: In the beginning of the century these were popular with wealthy Russian families. Now everyone has one. It is the triumph of socialism that in every single house in Soviet Union you find these now. (*He begins to open the nesting doll.*)

YOLANDA: I love it.

STEPAN: I bring you each one. You open the inside and there is another one. Perfect size. For you. (*He gives this second one to a guest.*) Then you go ahead and open third and there it is. For you? (*He gives a third one away.*) It's like little personalities we keep hidden away and no one knows about them, but then someone comes along and... Tada! (*He gives a fourth one away. The doll is quite small now.*) Nothing you keep inside now. Everything can be found. It only takes time. In Soviet Union there are no secrets anymore. Secrets are enemy of state. You can find everything if you use enough pressure. This tiny one is for you. (*He gives the smallest one to* CARMEN.) My hands empty. Magic. I have broken individual. Looked inside them and discovered everything. That's it. That's show.

(*Everyone applauds.*)

(*Then we hear voices offstage calling for* CARMEN.)

CARMEN: They're arriving. Let's get settled around the table.

ALVARO: Lead the way.

(*They all exit except* EMILIO *and* STEPAN.)

STEPAN: You're not coming.

EMILIO: I'll be right there.

STEPAN: Comrade?

EMILIO: What?

STEPAN: My job is to look over the people whose job it is to look over everyone else.

EMILIO: Say that again.

STEPAN: I keep an eye on your wife and Alvaro while they keep an eye on everyone else.

EMILIO: (*Playfully*) And who keeps an eye on you?

(STEPAN *shrugs.*)

STEPAN: I don't know. For all I know it's you. (*Pause*) Is it you?

EMILIO: Me?

STEPAN: Are you keeping an eye on me?

EMILIO: No, I am not keeping an eye on you. I am keeping both eyes on you.

STEPAN: Both eyes.

EMILIO: Both eyes. All eyes. And ears. Yes, my ears as well.

STEPAN: You're all in as they say.

EMILIO: Yes. *Salud.* (*He toasts.*)

STEPAN: *Salud. Salud.*

EMILIO: *Salud.*

(STEPAN *exits.*)

(EMILIO *puts his glass down. He starts to exit but stops. He knows there's someone else in the room with him.*)

(EMILIO *turns around. Standing there is* MARIA. *She wears a waitress uniform.*)

MARIA: You don't have to say anything. I know I'm a little underdressed for the party but your daughter has all my dresses.

(*Offstage we hear laughter, the sounds of a party.*)

MARIA: You know something though. No matter what she wears she can never be one of the beautiful people. (*She extends her arm.*) Go ahead. Escort me to my seat.

(EMILIO *doesn't move.*)

MARIA: What are you waiting for? You've seen me around. You know you want to touch me.

(EMILIO *walks up to* MARIA. *He touches her hair. This excites and terrifies him.*)

(CARMEN *enters.*)

CARMEN: What are you doing? We're waiting for you.

(*There's laughter offstage.*)

(*Lights fade quickly to black. Last light on the empty globe stand*)

(*We hear a snippet of Carlos Puebla once again singing Varadero.*)

(*Blackout*)

END OF ACT ONE

ACT TWO

Scene One

(*Another part of the house*)

(*The room is almost empty. There's a picture of the young girl we saw at the end of the act, near her a candle.*)

(EMILIO *is cleaning a gun.*)

CARMEN: (*Offstage*) I don't see anything.

EMILIO: She was there.

(CARMEN *enters.*)

CARMEN: The whole time at the table you weren't eating you looked so serious. I didn't know what had changed.

EMILIO: She was there.

CARMEN: There's nothing there now.

(YOLANDA *appears at the window. This should frighten us for a second.*)

YOLANDA: I walked all around. Nothing.

CARMEN: Come inside.

(YOLANDA *goes.*)

CARMEN: Look; you were drinking the whole night—

EMILIO: Don't tell me—

CARMEN: But it's true. You probably saw something move outside and you've been talking so much about seeing people—

EMILIO: This girl.

CARMEN: Seeing this girl—.

(YOLANDA *enters.*)

EMILIO: I know what I saw.

YOLANDA: What are you doing?

EMILIO: It needed to be clean. It's been a while.

YOLANDA: You're not allowed to have a gun in the house?

EMILIO: (*To* CARMEN) Are you going to write it up?

CARMEN: *Ay,* Emilio, *por fabor.*

(EMILIO *starts to go.*)

CARMEN: Where are you going?

EMILIO: I'm going to look for her. (*He goes.*)

YOLANDA: What do you think he intends to do with a gun if he finds a ghost?

CARMEN: Your father doesn't think things through.

YOLANDA: You better hope people don't find out he has a gun.

CARMEN: Did you see a gun?

YOLANDA: I just want—

CARMEN: Did you see one just now?

YOLANDA: In school they tell us everyone should have given up their guns by now.

CARMEN: I didn't see a gun. Did you?

(YOLANDA *shakes her head no.*)

CARMEN: Then don't ever mention one again.

YOLANDA: I wonder what he really saw?

(EMILIO *enters with a stack of cocktail dresses.*)

EMILIO: I want all of these out of the house.

YOLANDA: I'm not going to give these up.

CARMEN: Just listen to him so that this thing he believes is here goes away.

YOLANDA: These dresses belong to me. (*She spits on the candle and turns it off.*)

EMILIO: They belonged to this girl and maybe she'll finally go away if—

YOLANDA: If what? When does it stop? When we move out? When we move back home? She decided to go. I'm not having these people take back their house just because suddenly they miss home.

EMILIO: You're not sleeping in your room with those dresses.

YOLANDA: I'm not getting rid of them.

EMILIO: We'll keep them here until I figure out what to do with them.

YOLANDA: These are mine now.

EMILIO: I'm going to sleep here tonight. You go to bed now.

(*Beat*)

(YOLANDA *exits.*)

(CARMEN *walks up to the window and looks outside.*)

CARMEN: Gabriella is still awake. This book they showed me. Most women prefer sex with the lights off but she doesn't seem to mind. I wish I could live like that—like not caring who's watching. Just doing your own thing and not worrying about anyone. She's free.

EMILIO: Free because she doesn't turn off her lights?

CARMEN: Free because she has someone there to share something with.(*Beat*) Why don't you finally come to bed with me?

EMILIO: People are afraid of you.

CARMEN: Why?

EMILIO: They're jealous of this house, of us. It used to be that after work I'd go out with friends. Now no one asks me. They're afraid they'll say something wrong and that I'll tell you and they'll end up being questioned or worse. After work I sit in the park. Alone. I watch people. I wait till the sun goes down and I come home.

CARMEN: Lonely?

EMILIO: Yes.

CARMEN: I feel that way every night alone in that bed. (*She continues to look out the window.*) I know that you're having an affair. I know who it's with. When they gave us this house I thought that would put us far from where we were. It was only ten blocks but for me I thought...it's more than ten blocks. It's another world. This house is another world. But you've managed to bring our old world with you. I'm asking you to let it go and come to bed. (*Beat*) I'll wait up for you.

EMILIO: Don't.

CARMEN: Why are you doing this to me?

(EMILIO *doesn't answer.*)

(CARMEN *goes.*)

Scene Two

(A crowded gymnasium. STEPAN *stands in front of a giant washer/dryer. From the side* CARMEN *observes the audience.)*

STEPAN: In 1959 Richard Nixon showed to Soviet modern American house. With washer and dryer. He confuses washer and dryer with power. We have power. But we also have washer/dryer. Nixon thinks this washer of his is better than anything we can make. So we put our strongest scientists and physicists behind Project Combine. Project Combine was several years in development and we bring you here today what it is.

Historically Americans use both washer and dryer, but Project Combine takes that basic concept and combines the two. Here's how the Petronov machine works. In past you take clothes, you wet, you wash, and then it spins quickly removing all water but keeping clothes wet. The labor of the masses then remove wet clothes and put in second machine to dry. This presents many problems including space, time, cost. The men behind Project Combine have created tilting axis so that one machine can do both without woman having to watch and wait for transfer of clothes. When clothes are washed, the machine's axis tilts and the drying begins. The future is more automatic, less use of the woman to work so that she can then work for the building of Communist state.

Comrades, we not only protect you but help you through a more efficient than ever spin cycle.

(Lights shift.)

CARMEN: Committee to Defend the Revolution Report. January 20, 1962.

Today Compañero Stepan presented the people of Sancti-Spiritus with six washer/dryers. A few times during his important speech the audience stood and applauded for several minutes. He was pleased and felt very welcomed in our town as he told me later.

(*Light on* STEPAN)

STEPAN: I was pleased and felt very welcomed.

CARMEN: Wilfredo was late in releasing the balloons at the end of Stepan's speech but he later explained that because of all the applause he did not know when he was supposed to do it. After a while, the applause stopped and the delegates that were visiting from La Habana stayed on stage waiting for the balloons. People started to go home and the delegates did not know what to do. When the balloons were finally released everyone returned to their seats expecting the event to continue but there was nothing else. Nobody knew whether to go or to stay. Wilfredo apologized afterwards and he no longer wishes to be part of the Celebration Committee.

There were people missing from the event and those names are listed below.

(*Lights shift.*)

(ALVARO's *office*)

(ALVARO *and* STEPAN *are there with* CARMEN.)

ALVARO: Thank you for coming by. I enjoyed the party at your house the other night.

CARMEN: I'm glad.

STEPAN: Your husband is in very good mood.

CARMEN: He usually is.

STEPAN: Really?

CARMEN: Yes.

ALVARO: That's usually the kind of mood he's in?

CARMEN: Sometimes.

(*Pause*)

ALVARO: This last report you gave me, his name is not on the list.

CARMEN: My husband's name?

ALVARO: Your husband's name. Yes.

(ALVARO *shows* CARMEN *the report.*)

STEPAN: You should put his name down.

CARMEN: Why?

ALVARO: He wasn't there yesterday.

CARMEN: I thought I saw him there.

ALVARO: You thought you saw your husband—

CARMEN: Yes.

STEPAN: You saw a ghost then.

CARMEN: What?

ALVARO: Your husband was missing.

CARMEN: I'm sure—

ALVARO: You're not the only one in town I have writing reports for me. Your husband's name was listed as one who missed the event.

CARMEN: I thought—

ALVARO: You're sticking to your story?

(*Beat*)

CARMEN: I'll ask him.

ALVARO: Well it's not a big deal, is it?

CARMEN: No. I guess—

ALVARO: Is it?

CARMEN: I don't know what—

STEPAN: He probably wasn't feeling well.

CARMEN: I don't know.

STEPAN: Has someone come talk to you about me?

CARMEN: What do you mean?

STEPAN: To watch over me—is he watching me?

CARMEN: Why would my husband be watching you?

ALVARO: A group of mercenaries, traitors are hiding in the mountains near Santa Clara. Is your husband somehow connected to them?

CARMEN: Of course not!

ALVARO: Does he keep tabs on Stepan?

CARMEN: My husband? That's ridiculous.

STEPAN: He threatened me.

CARMEN: Oh, no. I'm sure—what did he say?

STEPAN: He said he had his eyes and ears both on me.

CARMEN: It was a joke I'm sure.

STEPAN: You find that humorous?

CARMEN: It just doesn't sound like my husband.

STEPAN: "A lie told often enough becomes the truth." He keeps repeating lie I will believe he watches me. I do not like being watched.

ALVARO: He does not like being watched.

CARMEN: If you want I can talk to him—

ALVARO: You mustn't. I'm having him questioned.

CARMEN: But—

ALVARO: You will not tell him about this conversation. I'm not sure who he is but I intend to find out.

CARMEN: You have the wrong person.

ALVARO: Good. Then you must know who the right person is.

CARMEN: No...but. Well there's no right person.

ALVARO: He no longer does volunteer work on Sundays.

CARMEN: My husband?

STEPAN: Last three Sundays he has missed volunteer work.

CARMEN: It's volunteer.

ALVARO: Yes it is.

CARMEN: It's not something you have to do.

STEPAN: It is imperative to volunteer.

(*Beat*)

CARMEN: He's been having trouble sleeping. I'm sure when he feels better—

ALVARO: What's keeping him awake?

STEPAN: Guilt.

CARMEN: What?

STEPAN: I sleep eight hours a day and I am perfectly regular. Is he regular?

CARMEN: I don't know really. You want me to find out if my husband is—

ALVARO: What's keeping him awake?

CARMEN: Living in a new house, adjusting to the place.

STEPAN: He has a lot on his mind.

CARMEN: Yes.

ALVARO: He threatened Stepan. Your husband knows more than he's letting on.

CARMEN: I am sure it was a misunderstanding.

ALVARO: More than maybe he's told you. Is that the case?

(Beat)

STEPAN: Your country was under imperialist attack not less than a year ago. I am not here to teach your country how to deal with laundry but how to find people that are not loyal. There are many still here waiting for a second attack to come. If that includes your husband then you must tell us.

CARMEN: Why would my husband say anything to you if he was—

STEPAN: He didn't realize how I was listening to him. There are men who enjoy walking right up to that line and looking over to see the precipice. They enjoy the feeling they get from danger. The feeling of being superior to the rest of us. The night of the party he walked up to that line but I happened to be very clear headed. He thought he was smarter than me but I have been watching people twenty years. I play the fool so that I am not so easily fooled.

ALVARO: Carmen. Do you think he knows more than he's shared with you?

CARMEN: *(Shaking her head no)* I don't know.

ALVARO: That's better. This is a good place to begin. *(Beat)* I want to inform you that his friend Flores with the American cigarettes—we picked up some letters that were intended for him.

CARMEN: He's not really friends with Flores.

ALVARO: They sometimes shoot pool together.

CARMEN: Sometimes but—

ALVARO: Flores's nephew worked for the Richard Nixon Election Committee in South Florida.

CARMEN: I don't know what that is.

ALVARO: I hope that when the time comes I can trust you to do the right thing. *(He starts to lead CARMEN out.)*

Let me ask you one more thing. You knew about his skipping Sundays. Not showing up for volunteer work. You knew he was doing that. Why didn't you put that information in any of your reports?

(*Beat*)

CARMEN: No.

ALVARO: What?

CARMEN: I didn't know.

(*Beat*)

ALVARO: Stepan, may I have a moment with...

(STEPAN *exits.*)

ALVARO: I'm sorry. He seems to be keeping secrets from both of us. I'm sorry that you're the last one to find out. Would you like a glass of water.

(CARMEN *shakes her head no.*)

ALVARO: Can I get you anything? Sit down. Carmen. Are you all right?

CARMEN: She may be involved.

ALVARO: Who?

CARMEN: My husband's ex-wife. She may be involved in the whole thing. For all I know it's her. It's probably just her. I know my husband has nothing to do with it. I know it's her. And if he's skipping Sundays it's because he's trying to stop her from being involved against this government.

ALVARO: Slow down. I need a name.

CARMEN: Josefina Lourdes Vega. Before I met my husband he was married to her—briefly. She's never been able to get over the divorce. When we moved to this new house I thought we would be far enough from her—she lives on the other side of town. There we used

to run into her quite a lot but I don't see her anymore.
He still sees her. He still visits her. She's involved.

ALVARO: Involved in what?

CARMEN: She has family in Santa Clara. Some of her
family was part of the Batista government. I believe
she's involved with them—with trying to stop the
change that's happening.

ALVARO: But you don't know for sure.

CARMEN: I do. I do know for sure. I haven't put it in
the reports but—well she has...she has...her family is
in Florida. She has told people in the neighborhood
that in Florida every house has air conditioner and
that the power does not go out at night and that cars...
there are highways and there's always milk...and it's
not powdered unless you're poor. And then one time
she said, "We're all poor here we just don't know
it because we have no one different around us to
compare ourselves to."

(ALVARO *stops writing.*)

ALVARO: Not enough.

CARMEN: What?

ALVARO: There's not enough there.

CARMEN: She is involved.

ALVARO: I don't believe you.

CARMEN: I didn't make those things up.

ALVARO: I don't think you made them up. I believe
those are things your husband has said.

CARMEN: No.

ALVARO: Yes.

CARMEN: Yes.

(*Pause*)

ALVARO: Can I ask you something, Carmen? Something perhaps—I want to ask you something personal.

CARMEN: What?

ALVARO: When did you and your husband last have intimate relations?

(CARMEN *cries. It's subtle.*)

(*Pause*)

ALVARO: May I have the book? The report I asked you to read.

(CARMEN *removes it from her purse.*)

ALVARO: You have told me what's happening in everyone's bedroom. Now I want you to tell me what's happening in yours.

(*Beat*)

CARMEN: Nothing.

(CARMEN *gives* ALVARO *the book.*)

ALVARO: We've known about the affair. I'm sorry this is the way you had to find out.

(ALVARO *reaches out to* CARMEN.)

CARMEN: I knew. I even told him I knew.(*Beat*)

I was lying. I didn't know.

(CARMEN *is in* ALVARO's *arms now. After a moment, she kisses him. She takes a step back and begins undressing.*)

(*Lights shift.*)

Scene Three

(MARIA, *seventeen, sits in the living room.* EMILIO *watches her go through her dresses. Her picture is still up, along with a candle.*)

MARIA: I wore this at my cousin's quinceñera. See the neckline? It's almost off the shoulder—almost. It was the first time I was able to show so much. Almost. Since really I didn't show anything. It's almost more of a square neckline but I felt so...like a woman. This dress right here—there was a shawl with it. Mami had one just like it. She was so sophisticated. I loved her dress so she had them make me one that was similar, but the one time I wore it to a wedding I lost the shawl and I never wore it again. Oh, look. My ballerina dress. Look at the length...like a bell. Terrific for dancing a waltz.

(EMILIO *whistles a waltz.* MARIA *dances for him. He joins her. He is scared and fascinated with the girl.*)

MARIA: I love all my dresses. They remind of all these special places and special memories. When you had that party the other night...then I knew for sure I was finally home. I heard the music and I knew you now accepted me. You were telling me to come in. To once again make myself at home. My father loves to throw parties. He loves people enjoying themselves. He throws so many parties. It's why I own so many different dresses.

EMILIO: I didn't know what I was going to do with them but you can have them. You can take them back with you.

MARIA: I don't want them.

EMILIO: They're yours.

MARIA: I know that.

EMILIO: Take them out of here. No one here wants them. Take them back with you.

MARIA: I haven't come back just for the dresses.

EMILIO: What do you mean?

MARIA: I've come back for everything.

EMILIO: You're taking everything back with you?

MARIA: I'm here to stay. I can't get used to the cold.

EMILIO: It's cold in Hialeah?

MARIA: It's a touch further from the equator. We really can't get used to it.

EMILIO: Oh.

MARIA: And all day I smell like fried fish. I work as a waitress at a restaurant called The Hungry Pelican. My dad is the manager and my mom is the hostess. We do everything except own the place. Here we used to own a restaurant but never go there. I don't like the smell of fried fish we bring home every night. A few weeks ago, I walked into the ocean. It was night but I wanted to wash the smells off of my body...inside my body. Soon I was swimming in the darkness. Then I saw the light from the coast and now here I am.

EMILIO: I think you're dead.

MARIA: What?

EMILIO: I think you drowned.

MARIA: What makes you say such a terrible thing?

EMILIO: The color of your face.

(MARIA *slaps* EMILIO.)

MARIA: I'm taking these back to my room. I'll wait in there. For an apology. (*She takes her dresses and exits.*)

(EMILIO *is alone on stage. He dances. He whistles. He is confused.*)

(*After a few moments,* YOLANDA *enters.*)

YOLANDA: What are you doing trying to get into my room?

EMILIO: What?

YOLANDA: When the door is locked it means you stay away. You kept trying to get in.

EMILIO: When?

YOLANDA: Just now. Stop it. Don't ever do that again. (*She goes. After a moment she comes back.*) I need help. The door is stuck.

EMILIO: Stuck?

YOLANDA: I can't get in. I didn't lock it. I don't know what happened.

EMILIO: Why don't you move to another room?

YOLANDA: Now?

EMILIO: I'll help you.

YOLANDA: You want to give this imaginary girl everything.

EMILIO: I just want her to have her room. Maybe then she'll leave me alone.

YOLANDA: She doesn't exist.

EMILIO: Then move out of your room for a while.

YOLANDA: I want my room. If you think she's in there get her out.

(YOLANDA *exits followed by* EMILIO.)

(*Immediately,* MARIA *enters and begins to open the French doors. The moment she steps into the room the ceiling fans come on.*)

(*Offstage we hear knocking.*)

EMILIO: (*Offstage*) Hello? Hello in there? I want you to meet my daughter.

(*More knocking*)

YOLANDA: (*Offstage*) Get out of my room, Maria!

EMILIO: (*Offstage*) Maria?

YOLANDA: (*Offstage*) If it's the same girl that's her name. I've read her diary.

EMILIO: (*Offstage*) Maria, give us a chance. Let my daughter see you.

(*By this time* MARIA *is sitting down comfortably.*)

EMILIO: (*Offstage*) Let us in. Come on. Open the door now.

YOLANDA: (*Offstage*) I want my room back!

MARIA: It's my room!

(*Long pause*)

EMILIO: (*Offstage*) Did you hear that?

(EMILIO *and* YOLANDA *enter.*)

YOLANDA: (*Softly*) Coño.

(EMILIO *and* YOLANDA *sit down and look at* MARIA.)

(*Lights shift.*)

Scene Four

(*The living room*)

(*The picture of the girl remains on with several candles near it.*)

(CARMEN *is on stage putting clear glasses of water on the shelves. She takes a cigar and blows smoke from it around the doors of the room.*)

(*After a moment,* YOLANDA *enters.*)

YOLANDA: Where are all my things?

CARMEN: Not now, Yolanda.

YOLANDA: What did you do with them?

CARMEN: Your father is not well.

YOLANDA: I'm not talking about my father. I'm talking about my new room—all my things are missing.

CARMEN: They weren't really yours.

YOLANDA: I want them put back.

CARMEN: I'll get you new things. I'll make you whatever you want.

(*Not really paying attention,* YOLANDA *takes a glass and drinks.*)

YOLANDA: I want what I already have.

CARMEN: Don't drink that?

YOLANDA: What's in it?

CARMEN: Water.

YOLANDA: So?

CARMEN: It's not for you.

YOLANDA: Why not?

CARMEN: You need to lower your voice. Now put it down.

YOLANDA: Who's going to hear me?

CARMEN: I only moved the dresses out of your new room for your father.

YOLANDA: What do you mean?

CARMEN: He's losing his mind. He thinks he sees—

YOLANDA: A ghost. I know.

CARMEN: I wanted to keep that room just the way it was right after we moved in. Maybe then your father will stop thinking he sees things.

YOLANDA: I see her too.

CARMEN: You?

YOLANDA: Sure.

CARMEN: You see the same girl your father sees?

YOLANDA: We spoke to her.

CARMEN: You did?

YOLANDA: The three of us sat down and made a deal. She could come back and have her old room if I got to keep the dresses in my new room.

CARMEN: You had a conversation with a ghost?

YOLANDA: Yes.

CARMEN: Why didn't anyone tell me?

YOLANDA: Isn't it your job to know everything?

CARMEN: Yes.

YOLANDA: Then you need to do a better job.

CARMEN: What was deal exactly?

YOLANDA: She told me I could keep the dresses. She told me I could have whatever I wanted in her room. All I needed to do was let her come back. Now if she's asking for her dresses back think about what she's going to want next. As soon as she gets the dresses, she's going to want this room and then the kitchen. Soon she's going to want the whole house. Are we going to let her have it? What was this whole Revolution about if we're now just going to compromise.

CARMEN: The water is to get rid of her.

YOLANDA: Oh. (*She puts down the glass.*)

(EMILIO *enters.*)

EMILIO: They came by work today.

CARMEN: Are you all right?

EMILIO: I don't feel well.

YOLANDA: What's wrong?

(EMILIO *starts to leave.*)

CARMEN: Where are you going?

EMILIO: Lie down. I'm exhausted.

CARMEN: Yoly told me you made some kind of deal with the young girl. When were you going to tell me?

EMILIO: I wasn't sure—

YOLANDA: I'm going to go find her in her room and make sure she understands the deal. (*She goes.*)

(*Beat*)

(EMILIO *starts to go.*)

CARMEN: Where do you go on Sundays?

EMILIO: She's inside the house. I don't want to leave Yolanda alone.

CARMEN: When you leave the house on Sundays, you go somewhere else.

EMILIO: I let her back in. It's my fault.

CARMEN: Listen to me. Where do you go?

EMILIO: I volunteer.

CARMEN: I know for a fact you don't.

EMILIO: Then if you know so much why are you asking me?

CARMEN: You go see her. You go see your ex-wife.

EMILIO: No.

CARMEN: I need to know the truth.

EMILIO: I don't.

CARMEN: Stop lying to me.

EMILIO: I'm not.

CARMEN: Reports have been filed. Other people are starting to write things down about you. One thing is me knowing. I feel like such a fool. Me. Of all people in the world I should have been the first to know. How long have you been seeing her?

EMILIO: Carmen.

CARMEN: I don't want the whole world knowing that you are back with her.

EMILIO: Who is telling you this?

CARMEN: Never mind who. The truth is—

EMILIO: I go home.

CARMEN: Home?

EMILIO: Every Sunday I go back to our old home. That's all I do. It's empty. I go there. I close my eyes and I fall asleep. I sleep all day long. I sleep because I can. I sleep because that house—however small it is—that house is ours.

(Beat)

CARMEN: Home?

(EMILIO nods yes.)

CARMEN: You're not seeing your ex-wife? *(Beat. She sits down.)* I'm sorry.

(Beat)

EMILIO: They asked me some questions today. They asked me to explain what I meant when I told Stepan that I had my eye on him.

(Lights shift.)

(STEPAN and ALVARO are there.)

STEPAN: A joke?

ALVARO: A funny joke?

EMILIO: I was a little drunk.

ALVARO: Ha ha joke?

EMILIO: What?

ALVARO: That kind of joke? Ha ha. Or one that you only laugh inside.

EMILIO: I don't know. I don't remember saying it.

STEPAN: Make me laugh again.

EMILIO: How?

ALVARO: Try another one.

EMILIO: Another joke?

STEPAN: You are funny man. Please make me laugh.

EMILIO: I don't know any jokes.

STEPAN: Everyone knows one joke.

ALVARO: He's right.

EMILIO: I don't really—

ALVARO: You see now I think you're lying.

STEPAN: Alvaro knows joke. I know joke. Your wife— we have spoken to her—she knows joke.

ALVARO: He's right. Tell us a joke.

(Beat)

EMILIO: Three women are sitting on their porch. One says I love the Revolution because now I get everything I want. The second woman says I love the Revolution because now I am finally working. The third woman says in the Revolution I now get fucked harder than ever. The two women look at the third woman surprised and ask, How does the Revolution help you do this? The third woman says, I have to clean the house, do the laundry, work in the mill, and volunteer all my free time. The two women then ask in unison. Yes, but how does that help you to get fucked?

(EMILIO *waits for a laugh. He sees that it's not coming.*)

(*Long pause*)

ALVARO: Stepan, do you think that's funny?

STEPAN: I am like the two women because I don't understand how that helps third woman to get fucked.

ALVARO: You see you need to explain it. And if you need to explain it it's not funny. Who taught you this joke?

EMILIO: I just heard it.

ALVARO: From whom?

EMILIO: Around. It was just...I don't know.

ALVARO: I need a name.

(*Beat*)

EMILIO: No.

ALVARO: A name.

EMILIO: No.

ALVARO: Give me a name.

EMILIO: Emilio Montes Busto.

(*Beat*)

ALVARO: Sign this piece of paper.

(EMILIO *does.*)

ALVARO: That's all we need for now.

(*Lights shift.*)

(STEPAN *and* ALVARO *go.*)

(EMILIO *opens his arms to reach out to* CARMEN. *He's very vulnerable. She takes a few steps toward him but she stops.*)

EMILIO: Carmen.

CARMEN: I wanted a new life.

EMILIO: I'm sorry.

CARMEN: I saw her from the very beginning. The very first day we moved in. I pretended not to see her. I was in my room looking at myself in the mirror and I saw a figure outside the window. I didn't even look back. Instead I chose to close my eyes. I closed my eyes because for this kind of life you need to go forward with your eyes closed.(*She goes.*)

(*Lights shift.*)

Scene Five

(*The living room*)

(ALVARO, EMILIO, *and* YOLANDA)

(EMILIO *is handing over his gun.*)

ALVARO: *Armas para que?*

EMILIO: I've always owned one.

ALVARO: All over the radio, the newspaper you hear the same question. Arms for what? *Armas para que?*

(STEPAN *enters from the kitchen eating a mango.*)

ALVARO: All guns and rifles are being collected. You should have been first in line to turn your gun in.

(CARMEN *enters.*)

ALVARO: Unless. Unless there was a reason why you didn't want to.

YOLANDA: He didn't think—

ALVARO: He didn't think or he didn't want to.

(*Beat*)

EMILIO: I didn't want to.

(MARIA *enters.* ALVARO *and* STEPAN *do not see her.*)

ALVARO: That's the first thing you've said today that I believe.

CARMEN: Why did you say that?

ALVARO: I think you've forgotten something, Carmen. Today I'm asking the questions.

EMILIO: It only has one bullet.

ALVARO: What?

EMILIO: I only kept one bullet.

STEPAN: Very poetic. I'd do the same if I were married to dangerous woman.

EMILIO: It was for me. They have nothing to do with the gun.

ALVARO: I want you all to get your things together as soon as possible.

CARMEN: Where are you moving us?

ALVARO: I am not in the real estate business. I suppose they'll move you around for a while. Then they'll find you the most uncomfortable place in the world and there you'll land with the knowledge of what comfort really was.

MARIA: I hope they send you to Hialeah.

ALVARO: I want everything collected. Do not remove anything that doesn't belong to you.

MARIA: That's right.

(ALVARO *hesitates before continuing. Did he hear something?* MARIA *goes but soon returns through another door.*)

ALVARO: You're walking out the same way you walked in. We'll be checking everything.

EMILIO: (*Overlapping*) You can have it.

ALVARO: What?

CARMEN: He's been trying to give it back to you for the past three months.

(ALVARO *nods at* STEPAN.)

STEPAN: You must be out in two hours.

CARMEN: We don't need that much time.

(*Everyone rises.*)

YOLANDA: Who are you moving in here next?

STEPAN: I am.

YOLANDA: You're taking this house?

STEPAN: How is the plumbing? In Soviet Union we have only one problem that has come to my attention. During the winter months—that is to say most of the year—pipes freeze and problem with plumbing is frequent.

YOLANDA: You probably won't have that problem here.

STEPAN: Good. I have now decided to stay indefinitely.

MARIA: If he thinks he's staying here he's got another thing coming.

STEPAN: The washer/dryer might break down. It may need my assistance. I will call the Kremlin for help. Hello, Kremlin. They will hear the seriousness of my voice and send immediate assistance. They will send help. It will be very easy to respond to any American aggression if I am here.

YOLANDA: What do Americans care how we do our laundry?

STEPAN: American aggression extends to everything. Already we are moving in and building base for future attack protection. I must be here present for future.

ALVARO: Now get your things.

STEPAN: Stay. Yolanda. For a moment.

(*Everyone exits except* MARIA, YOLANDA, *and* STEPAN.)

STEPAN: Personally what is happening to you is because of Papa. I wish my hands were not tied. I hope you understand I feel much for you.(*He gets closer.*) This does not change anything. What happened at the party is real. I want you to visit. I feel there's still more remaining to do.

(YOLANDA *walks away from* STEPAN. *He stops her forcefully.*)

STEPAN: Do not ruin your life.

YOLANDA: You're not going to like it here.

STEPAN: Is that so? I like it here already.

YOLANDA: You'll leave soon.

(STEPAN *is still holding on to* YOLANDA.)

STEPAN: I'll leave when I want.

(STEPAN *kisses* YOLANDA. *She lets herself be kissed— not because she wants to but because she is momentarily paralyzed. Then...*)

YOLANDA: (*To* MARIA) Why aren't you doing anything? Do something to him.

(MARIA *looks on as* STEPAN *holds on to* YOLANDA.)

STEPAN: Oh dear. Has my kiss made you lose your mind already.

YOLANDA: (*To* MARIA) What are you waiting for? Show him that you're here.

STEPAN: I fear you will throw yourself in front of train if you don't let me help.

(STEPAN *tries to kiss* YOLANDA *again.*)

YOLANDA: You don't see her?

STEPAN: Who?

YOLANDA: Her. She's a ghost.

(*All three ceiling fans come on.*)

STEPAN: Who's that?

YOLANDA: The girl who lived here. She's standing in front of you.

STEPAN: A ghost?

(MARIA *is waving her hand in front of* STEPAN.)

STEPAN: I'm a Marxist-Leninist. As a matter of political belief, I am unable to see ghosts.

(*All three ceiling fans go off.*)

(STEPAN *goes.*)

YOLANDA: He's not going to be as easy to get rid of.

MARIA: I will figure out a way of making myself visible to him. Don't you have to finish packing?

YOLANDA: I don't really have much. I left most of my old stuff behind because I knew things here would be nicer.

MARIA: I can't say that I'm going to miss you.

YOLANDA: What was it like when you had to leave?

MARIA: Nothing really special.

YOLANDA: Tell me.

MARIA: My mother told me first. I was in the bath. She knocked on the door and came in. She said I'm going to tell you something. I said, I know. We're leaving. They thought they were keeping it from me. I'd go to bed at night, pretend to go to sleep, after a while I'd get up and go listen at their door. They argued about what they should do. All night. Should we go? Should we stay? I knew everything.

YOLANDA: But if you didn't really want to leave why didn't you say anything?

MARIA: Who said I didn't want to leave?

YOLANDA: You wanted to go?

MARIA: I've always been fooled by change. Ever since my body started to do things I've put too much faith in it. Do you know what I mean?

YOLANDA: Anywhere must be better than where you are.

MARIA: When it comes to you that's true but not for me. Too bad I didn't know that back then. In 1958 when everyone was wondering what was next I was so excited. You see up to that point so much had been expected of me—socially I mean. The dresses I had to wear. The people I had to talk to. The boy I had to marry. The boy I had to marry. I made the same mistake everyone made. I made the Revolution all about myself. I made it about all the freedom I'd have in my life, and then one day I found myself frying fish in Hialeah. What freedom!

(*Offstage we hear doors being opened and closed, a couple of suitcases being dragged, general activity, etc.*)

MARIA: One week of frying fish and I wanted to come back. They told me it would only be six months, maybe a year—an extended vacation. On New Year's Eve, my father said, Next Year in La Habana. I don't believe my father anymore. I don't think my father believes my father. That's why he's outside now waiting for you to leave so that he can come in.

YOLANDA: Your father?

MARIA: Yes.

YOLANDA: Why doesn't he just come in now like you did?

MARIA: He's too polite.

YOLANDA: So he's here?

MARIA: So is my mother and my uncle.

YOLANDA: They're here?

MARIA: Yes.

YOLANDA: Outside?

MARIA: Waiting for you to go. After I left they decided to follow me into the water. Funny thing is you find so many people at sea—floating. They all seem headed in one direction and we're headed in another.

(YOLANDA *goes and looks out the window.*)

YOLANDA: They're pretending not to be there.

MARIA: Just wave at them.

(YOLANDA *does.*)

MARIA: What are they doing now?

YOLANDA: Waving back.(*She continues to wave.*)

MARIA: What are they doing now?

YOLANDA: Still waving.

(CARMEN *walks in with a beat up suitcase and puts it on the floor.*)

CARMEN: Who are you waving at?

YOLANDA: Nobody.

CARMEN: (*Making sure the suitcase is closed*) I don't want you talking to her anymore.

YOLANDA: She was just telling me about her family.

MARIA: Your mother is right. The less personal this thing is the better.

CARMEN: Go find whatever is yours and make sure it's packed.

YOLANDA: I don't want to go.

CARMEN: That's just the way it is. Sometimes it's their turn, sometimes it's ours.

(YOLANDA *exits*.)

MARIA: You need me to sit on that so you can close it better?

(CARMEN *doesn't respond*.)

MARIA: You ought to think about getting new luggage.

CARMEN: I doubt we'll be moving around much after this.

MARIA: Probably true but you never know when that trip presents itself and then you suddenly have to go running to the store and they've run out of alligator skin. It can be terrible.

CARMEN: This isn't alligator skin so it won't be a problem.

MARIA: My mother taught me a lesson early on about cheap luggage. She said always buy the very best because then people will assume that what's inside is equally valuable. Of course that doesn't always work in your favor. When we were at the airport they didn't let us take our luggage on the plane because they assumed—quite correctly—that what we had in it was extremely valuable. All it was were books from when I was very little, some of my favorite toys....

CARMEN: That's it?

MARIA: And my mother's jewelry, of course.

CARMEN: Stand up.

MARIA: What?

CARMEN: I'm done.

MARIA: You sound a little upset.

CARMEN: Do I?

MARIA: Just a little.

CARMEN: I want to know how you did it.

MARIA: Did what?

CARMEN: How did you hold on to this?

MARIA: By not ever letting go. Every day we talked about it. Talked about it so much that it grew. It grew and grew in our minds until I just had to have it.

(EMILIO *enters with another piece of luggage—equally beat up. He stacks it on top of the other one.*)

MARIA: A matching set—how charming.

(CARMEN *struggles to close that second piece of luggage properly.*)

CARMEN: *Coño.*

EMILIO: Let me help you with that.

(CARMEN *continues to struggle with it.*)

EMILIO: Carmen? (*Beat*) I'm sorry.

CARMEN: We're never going to have it this nice again.

EMILIO: I'm going to work hard. I'm going to do everything. I'm going to get us to Hialeah.

CARMEN: I don't like you.

EMILIO: The change will be good...will be good for us. I promise.

CARMEN: Did you hear me?

EMILIO: Yes.

CARMEN: Look at what you're leaving. Look at it. Really look at everything you have now because you're never going to see it again.

(*Beat*)

EMILIO: You?

(CARMEN *now focuses all her attention on the luggage.*)

(YOLANDA *enters quickly—her face flushed.*)

EMILIO: Are you all right?

(YOLANDA *nods yes.*)

EMILIO: Are you sure?

(YOLANDA *remains up against one of the walls. She wants to disappear into it. She is visibly upset.*)

EMILIO: I promise I'll make this up to both of you.

CARMEN: I don't want you crying over this.

(YOLANDA *nods yes.*)

(STEPAN *enters holding a cocktail dress.* YOLANDA *takes a step back. He holds out the dress for her.*)

(ALVARO *enters.*)

ALVARO: Are you ready?

(YOLANDA *hesitates. She takes a step toward the dress but stops.*)

CARMEN: Just take it!

(YOLANDA *does.* EMILIO *exits.*)

MARIA: (*To* YOLANDA)

You have absolutely no taste. You've taken the one dress that will never come back into style.

(YOLANDA *leaves followed by* STEPAN.)

(MARIA *walks up to the record player and plays a song—* Varadero *comes on. She stops it and throws it aside. She puts on* Rompe Saraguey—*oldest version available.*)

ALVARO: Well?

CARMEN: Yes.

(ALVARO *and* CARMEN *dance for a moment. They kiss.*)

CARMEN: (*To* MARIA) I'll be seeing you again. I don't let go either.

(ALVARO *and* CARMEN *exit.*)

(MARIA *walks across the room, as she does she takes one quick dance step.*)

(MARIA *looks out the window and motions for her family to come in. She looks around.*)

(MARIA *starts to make it her home again while the lights begin a painfully slow fade and the music does an equally slow rise.*)

END OF PLAY